A MESSAGE TO GARCIA AND OTHER WORKS

By ELBERT HUBBARD

A Message to Garcia and Other Works
By Elbert Hubbard

Print ISBN 13: 978-1-4209-5523-1
eBook ISBN 13: 978-1-4209-5524-8

Cover Image: a detail of a photograph of Elbert Hubbard, c. 1904. Colorization by Erica Amaral, Digireads.com Publishing copyright 2017.

Please visit *www.digireads.com*

CONTENTS

Apologia

This literary trifle, *A Message to Garcia*, was written one evening after supper, in a single hour. It was on the Twenty-second of February, Eighteen Hundred Ninety-nine, Washington's Birthday, and we were just going to press with the March *Philistine*. The thing leaped hot from my heart, written after a trying day, when I had been endeavoring to train some rather delinquent villagers to abjure the comatose state and get radioactive.

The immediate suggestion, though, came from a little argument over the teacups, when my boy Bert suggested that Rowan was the real hero of the Cuban War.

Rowan had gone alone and done the thing —carried the message to Garcia.

It came to me like a flash! Yes, the boy is right, the hero is the man who does his work—who carries the message to Garcia.

I got up from the table, and wrote *A Message to Garcia*. I thought so little of it that we ran it in the Magazine with-out a heading. The edition went out, and soon orders began to come for extra copies of the March *Philistine*, a dozen, fifty, a hundred; and when the American News Company ordered a thousand, I asked one of my helpers which article it was that had stirred up the cosmic dust.

"It's the stuff about Garcia," he said.

The next day a telegram came from George H. Daniels, of the New York Central Railroad, thus "Give price on one hundred thousand Rowan article in pamphlet form—Empire State Express advertisement on back—also how soon can ship."

I replied giving price, and stated we could supply the pamphlets in two years. Our facilities were small and a hundred thousand booklets looked like an awful undertaking

The result was that I gave Mr. Daniels permission to reprint the article in his own way. He issued it in booklet form in editions of half a million. Two or three of these half-million lots were sent out by Mr. Daniels, and in addition the article was reprinted in over two hundred magazines and newspapers. It has been translated into all written languages.

At the time Mr. Daniels was distributing the *Message to Garcia*, Prince Hilakoff, Director of Russian Railways, was in this country. He was the guest of the New York Central, and made a tour of the country under the personal direction of Mr. Daniels. The, Prince saw the little book and was interested in it, more because Mr. Daniels was putting it out in such big numbers, probably, than otherwise.

In any event, when he got home he had the matter translated into Russian, and a copy of the booklet given to every railroad employee in

Russia.

Other countries then took it up, and from Russia it passed into Germany, France, Spain, Turkey, Hindustan and China. During the war between Russia and Japan, every Russian soldier who went to the front was given a copy of the *Message to Garcia*.

The Japanese, finding the booklets in possession of the Russian prisoners, concluded that it must be a good thing, and accordingly translated it into Japanese.

And on an order of the Mikado, a copy was given to every man in the employ of the Japanese Government, soldier or civilian.

Over forty million copies of *A Message to Garcia* have been printed. This is said to be a larger circulation than any other literary venture has ever attained during the lifetime of the author, in all history— thanks to a series of lucky accidents.

E. H., East Aurora, December 1, 1913.

A Message to Garcia

The Philistine, March 1899.

In all this Cuban business there is one man stands out on the horizon of my memory like Mars at perihelion.

When war broke out between Spain and the United States, it was very necessary to communicate quickly with the leader of the Insurgents. Garcia was somewhere in the mountain fastnesses of Cuba—no one knew where. No mail or telegraph message could reach him. The President must secure his co-operation, and quickly.

What to do!

Some one said to the President, "There is a fellow by the name of Rowan will find Garcia for you, if anybody can."

Rowan was sent for and given a letter to be delivered to Garcia. How the "fellow by the name of Rowan" took the letter, sealed it up in an oilskin pouch, strapped it over his heart, in four days landed by night off the coast of Cuba from an open boat, disappeared into the jungle, and in three weeks came out on the other side of the Island, having traversed a hostile country on foot, and delivered his letter to Garcia— are things I have no special desire now to tell in detail. The point that I wish to make is this: McKinley gave Rowan a letter to be delivered to Garcia; Rowan took the letter and did not ask, "Where is he at?"

By the Eternal! there is a man whose form should be cast in deathless bronze and the statue placed in every college of the land. It is not book-learning young men need, nor instruction about this and that, but a stiffening of the vertebrae which will cause them to be loyal to a trust, to act promptly, concentrate their energies: do the thing— "Carry a message to Garcia."

General Garcia is dead now, but there are other Garcias. No man who has endeavored to carry out an enterprise where many hands were needed, but has been well-nigh appalled at times by the imbecility of the average man—the inability or unwillingness to concentrate on a thing and do it.

Slipshod assistance, foolish inattention, dowdy indifference, and half-hearted work seem the rule; and no man succeeds, unless by hook or crook or threat he forces or bribes other men to assist him; or mayhap, God in His goodness performs a miracle, and sends him an Angel of Light for an assistant.

You, reader, put this matter to a test: You are sitting now in your office—six clerks are within call. Summon any one and make this request: "Please look in the encyclopedia and make a brief memorandum for me concerning the life of Correggio."

Will the clerk quietly say, "Yes, sir," and go do the task?

On your life he will not. He will look at you out of a fishy eye and ask one or more of the following questions:

Who was he?

Which encyclopedia?

Where is the encyclopedia?

Was I hired for that?

Don't you mean Bismarck?

What's the matter with Charlie doing it?

Is he dead?

Is there any hurry?

Sha'n't I bring you the book and let you look it up yourself?

What do you want to know for?

And I will lay you ten to one that after you have answered the questions, and explained how to find the information, and why you want it, the clerk will go off and get one of the other clerks to help him try to find Garcia—and then come back and tell you there is no such man. Of course I may lose my bet, but according to the Law of Average I will not. Now, if you are wise, you will not bother to explain to your "assistant" that Correggio is indexed under the C's, not in the K's, but you will smile very sweetly and say, "Never mind," and go look it up yourself. And this incapacity for independent action, this moral stupidity, this infirmity of the will, this unwillingness to cheerfully catch hold and lift—these are the things that put pure Socialism so far into the future. If men will not act for themselves, what will they do when the benefit of their effort is for all?

A first mate with knotted club seems necessary; and the dread of getting "the bounce" Saturday night holds many a worker to his place. Advertise for a stenographer, and nine out of ten who apply can neither spell nor punctuate—and do not think it necessary to.

Can such a one write a letter to Garcia?

"You see that bookkeeper," said the foreman to me in a large factory.

"Yes; what about him?"

"Well, he's a fine accountant, but if I'd send him up town on an errand, he might accomplish the errand all right, and on the other hand, might stop at four saloons on the way, and when he got to Main Street would forget what he had been sent for."

Can such a man be entrusted to carry a message to Garcia?

We have recently been hearing much maudlin sympathy expressed for the "downtrodden denizens of the sweatshop" and the "homeless wanderer searching for honest employment," and with it all often go many hard words for the men in power.

Nothing is said about the employer who grows old before his time in a vain attempt to get frowsy ne'er-do-wells to do intelligent work; and his long, patient striving after "help" that does nothing but loaf when his back is turned. In every store and factory there is a constant weeding-out process going on. The employer is constantly sending away "help" that have shown their incapacity to further the interests of the business, and others are being taken on. No matter how good times are, this sorting continues: only, if times are hard and work is scarce, the sorting is done finer—but out and forever out the incompetent and unworthy go. It is the survival of the fittest. Self-interest prompts every employer to keep the best—those who can carry a message to Garcia.

I know one man of really brilliant parts who has not the ability to manage a business of his own, and yet who is absolutely worthless to any one else, because he carries with him constantly the insane suspicion that his employer is oppressing, or intending to oppress, him. He can not give orders, and he will not receive them. Should a message be given him to take to Garcia, his answer would probably be, "Take it yourself!"

Tonight this man walks the streets looking for work, the wind whistling through his threadbare coat. No one who knows him dare employ him, for he is a regular firebrand of discontent. He is impervious to reason, and the only thing that can impress him is the toe of a thick-soled Number Nine boot.

Of course I know that one so morally deformed is no less to be pitied than a physical cripple; but in our pitying let us drop a tear, too, for the men who are striving to carry on a great enterprise, whose working hours are not limited by the whistle, and whose hair is fast turning white through the struggle to hold in line dowdy indifference, slipshod imbecility, and the heartless ingratitude which, but for their enterprise, would be both hungry and homeless.

Have I put the matter too strongly? Possibly I have; but when all the world has gone a-slumming I wish to speak a word of sympathy for the man who succeeds—the man who, against great odds, has directed the efforts of others, and having succeeded, finds there's nothing in it: nothing but bare board and clothes. I have carried a dinner-pail and worked for day's wages, and I have also been an employer of labor, and I know there is something to be said on both sides. There is no excellence, per se, in poverty; rags are no recommendation; and all employers are not rapacious and high-handed, any more than all poor men are virtuous. My heart goes out to the man who does his work when the "boss" is away, as well as when he is at home. And the man who, when given a letter for Garcia, quietly takes the missive, without asking any idiotic questions, and with no lurking intention of chucking it into the nearest sewer, or of doing aught else but deliver it, never gets "laid off," nor has to go on a strike for higher wages. Civilization is one long, anxious search for just such individuals. Anything such a man asks shall be granted. He is wanted in every city, town and village—in every office, shop, store and factory. The world cries out for such; he is needed and needed badly—the man who can "Carry a Message to Garcia."

Success

The Philistine, May, 1904.

The other day I asked a dear little girl, nine years old, what was the meaning of the word "success."

And without an instant's hesitation she answered: "It means to succeed—I thought everybody knew that!"

"To succeed in what?" I ventured.

"Why, in what you are trying to do, of course."

And I kissed the little girl once on the forehead and twice on her dimpled chin, and let it go at that.

But let it be assumed that there is no such thing as success in bad business. To succeed in injuring another would be a calamity for me—not a success. We all want to succeed in doing what will bring the best possible results to ourselves and the least possible harm to others. So success means, first, to achieve what is good for yourself. And, second, to do that which bestows a benefit on others.

And, of course, there are many degrees of success.

Let us once and forever get rid of the savage fallacy that success lies through sacrifice. The person who loves you so well that he will sacrifice himself for you will sacrifice you for others, if he loves you well enough. If martyrdom is a good thing for me, I'll visit it on you, if I can, for your own good. And thus we see that martyr and persecutor are cut off the same piece of cloth—and in the past they have shifted places with great alacrity. There is really small choice between them.

Success implies joy in your work—and joy means better work tomorrow. And all good work is reciprocal—it benefits many people.

But all success is comparative—no success is final. And the reason that success sometimes palls or embitters is because the person has sat down to enjoy it, not knowing that every success is a preparation for a greater success just ahead. You must gather your manna every day.

So far as we know, a successful life here is the best possible preparation for a successful life to come. And while there are no pockets in a shroud, yet the soul you have you'd better not barter clean away. The soul you have here will be the soul you have there—else is immortality vain. And whether this soul is "saved" or not will depend upon whether it is worth saving.

So the highest wisdom, it seems, would be the ambition to succeed in having a soul worth saving.

And to succeed in this ambition my advice would be, Don't trouble much about your soul—do not pull off the flowers to see how the roots are growing.

Do your work, and what you are will be shown in what you do.

Work is exercise, and exercise is expression. We grow only through exercise—we are strong in the muscles we use, and it is so with every faculty of the soul and every attribute of the mind. We are strong in the faculties we use.

And if all work is exercise, and we grow only through exercise, then the wisdom of exercising our highest and best will be at once apparent.

I am told that rabbits do not catch mice. And the idea has just come to me that the reason rabbits do not catch mice is because they do not desire to.

Perhaps I am wrong about this, but I have to say what I think.

Cats catch mice. A cat is no quicker in its movements than a rabbit and cannot run as fast, but the cat desires to catch mice, and does.

Yet, if you ever watched a cat about to spring upon a mouse, it never occurred to you that the cat had studied the problem; had revolved in its head all of the best methods for a spring, and worked out a theory for the most successful pounce.

No; the cat has no theories. The cat just catches the mouse, and while the rabbit is chewing the cud and theorizing, the fox catches the rabbit.

Things that chew the cud do not catch anything.

The objection can here be raised that in its nature the rabbit is not a mouse-catching animal; the cat is, and hence no praise nor blame can be accorded either way. All of which is very true. And this is where man has the advantage of cats and rabbits—he has the power of choice.

Of course, I am quite aware that some psychologists say that we merely succumb to the strongest attractions and call it choice, but the theory is a trifle too fine for the average brain, and fatalism as a religion went out with Schopenhauer.

Man can weigh, sift, consider, and decide—he makes a choice. I come to a point where the road forks—I decide which branch I will take. I may then follow it for a mile, and retrace my steps, and take the other track. And this ability to choose is what differentiates man from the brute.

You can do the wrong thing if you wish; if you desire to choose an absurd thing you may.

In his essay on "Compensation"—the best thing ever written by an American—Emerson says, "'What will you have,' quoth God—'pay the price!'"

After you have chosen what you want, before you can possess it you must pay the price.

Usually, the more valuable the thing the higher the price. The price is given only to those who deserve it—those who earn it.

The cat pays the price of the mouse by long hours of silent watching—in stealthy chase—personal comfort is never considered.

There is a oneness of aim—a complete concentration, and it is this singleness of purpose that brings the cat success.

It is about time, perhaps, to drop the metaphor, lest one of those forty thousand persons who daily cross London Bridge shall construe this into an argument favoring feline methods in winning success. And so I will here say that the stealthy, silent crouching and crawling, the lying in wait, and the sudden spring, are all right for cats, but for man there is a better way.

Success is the result of a mental attitude, and the right mental attitude will bring a success in everything you undertake.

In fact, there is no such thing as failure, excepting to those who accept and believe in failure. Failure! There is no such word in all the bright lexicon of speech unless you yourself have written it there.

A great success, as I have said before—and as I like to repeat—is made up of an aggregation of little ones. These finally form a segregation—a whole. The man who fills a position of great honor and great trust has first fulfilled many smaller positions of trust.

The man who has the superintendence of ten thousand men, say, like Mr. James J. Hill, has had the charge of many small squads.

And before he had charge of a small squad, he had charge of himself.

When he was a baggage-man he had charge of the baggage and he did his work so faithfully, so efficiently, so well that it was very soon discovered that he needed no superintendence.

The man who does his work so well that he needs no supervision has already succeeded.

And the acknowledgment of his success is sure to follow in the form of a promotion. And even should not promotion speedily follow, the man has gained power—grown in personality. He is more to himself—more to God. The world wants its work done, and civilization is simply a constant search for men who can do things.

Success is the most natural thing in the world. The man who does not succeed has placed himself in opposition to the laws of the universe. The world needs you—it wants what you can produce—you can serve it, and if you will, it will reward you richly.

By doing your work you are moving in line of least resistance—it is a form of self-protection. You need what others have to give—they need you.

To rebel is folly.

To reciprocate is wisdom.

To consume and not produce is a grave mistake, and upon such a one Nature will surely visit her displeasure.

The common idea is that success means great sacrifice and that you must buy it with a price. In one sense this is true.

To succeed you must choose. If you want this you cannot have that.

Success demands concentration—oneness of aim and desire.

Choose this day whom you will serve.

Paradoxically, it is true that you must "sacrifice" some things to gain others. If you are a young man and wish to succeed in business, you will have to sacrifice the cigarettes, the late hours, the dice, the cards, and all that round of genteel folly which saps your strength and tends to unfit you for your work tomorrow.

That awkward and uncouth country boy who went to work yesterday is concentrating on his tasks—he is doing the thing, high or low, menial or what not—yes! He is not so very clever, his trousers bag at the knee and his sleeves are too short, but his heart has but one desire—to do his work.

I am no prophet, nor the son of a prophet, but I'll tell you this God's truth: That uncouth country boy will someday be a partner in this firm, and you with your sharp ways, your cigarettes, your midnight suppers, and your smart clothes bought on the installment plan, will go to him and beg for favors which he alone can grant.

Why? Because he is in the line of evolution—he is growing and you are not. You are standing still, and to stand still is to retreat.

An ounce of loyalty is worth a pound of cleverness.

Astuteness adds nothing to the wealth of the world. The astute man is worth nothing to the community—all his astuteness is valuable for is to protect himself from other astute men. And his shrewdness and his astuteness so advertise themselves that nobody trusts him— nobody believes in him. This type of the sharp man is found in every community.

And so the habit of continually looking out for Number One is fatal to success. Nature is on her guard against such, and if by accident they get into a position of power their lease on the place is short.

A great success demands a certain abnegation—a certain disinterestedness.

The man who can lose himself in his work is the one who will succeed best.

Courtesy, kindness, and concentration—this trinity forms the sesame that will unlock all doors.

Good cheer is the direct concomitant of good health. Isn't it the part of wisdom not to put an enemy in your mouth to steal away your brains? Isn't it better not to know you have a stomach and to so fill your working hours that the night comes as a blessing and a benediction—a time for sweet rest and dreams?

These things mean a preparation for good work. And good work means a preparation for higher work.

Success is easy. You do not ascend the mountain by standing in the valley and jumping over it. Success is only difficult to the man who is trying to lift himself by tugging at his boot-straps.

You cross the mountain ranges of difficulty step by step. And all the way the scenery changes and is beautiful. Up you go, step by step, occasionally stopping to take a breath, now and again retracing steps to keep on the right path.

But forward and forward and upward and forever upward we go.

And having crossed this range, we know we shall be confronted with others beyond. But through the effort we are growing stronger— exercise gives power for more exercise. Exercise is expression, and expression is not only necessary to life—it is life.

We are not afraid. Much joy has been ours, and is ours. The past is safe. And finally should flesh falter, and we pause for rest, and out across the valley should we catch misty glimpses of peaks beyond, we are still unafraid, and firmly do we believe that the power which upheld us Here will not desert us There.

Life Lies in the Quest

The Philistine, November, 1904.

It is beautiful that parents should be filled with a desire to educate their children. Education means development—evolution, growth. Can you impart a development? I think not. One can, however, in degree, supply the Conditions of Growth.

We cannot make the plant blossom, but we can place it in the sunshine and supply it aliment and moisture.

The birds instruct their young about how to fly about, to secure food and to escape their enemies.

But when the young bird has grown to the size of its parents, can wing its way, and capture its own food, then the old one leaves it to work out its destiny alone. Humans should do the same. All sensible parents would like to have their children surpass them—do things they could never do, and overcome obstacles that were to them insurmountable.

And if this is to occur, the parents better cease pounding into the youth who has passed adolescence the idea that he should pattern his career after that of his Pa.

If men had always been satisfied with the religion of their mothers, and the science and economics of their fathers, we would still be in the dark ages—very dark.

College education, with the protective parental features, for a husky youth of nineteen, weight one hundred and eighty, is a dangerous and degenerating process. The marvel is that so many survive it, and turn out to be really useful citizens. Only the inherent goodness and virtue of men could ever live down such a handicap. Nature nowhere presents this parallel—of taking the full-grown young out of life in order to educate them for life.

The men in every line of useful effort who have made epochs, who stand for us as fixed stars, have never been subjected to this deteriorating process of fussy protection and futile overseeing. Let me name you these graduates of the University of Hard Knocks, who never attended any other, each of whom is King, by divine right, in his own particular specialty:

1. Shakespeare, in Literature.
2. Herbert Spencer, in Philosophy.
3. Abraham Lincoln, in Statesmanship.
4. Thomas A. Edison, Applied Science.
5. Benjamin Franklin, All-'Round Development.
6. Napoleon Bonaparte, Generalship.

7. Robert G. Ingersoll, Oratory.
8. Jean Francois Millet, Painting.
9. Augustus St. Gaudens, Sculpture.
10. James J. Hill, Finance.

The last name in this list stands peculiarly alone—the man built a railway across a continent and made it pay without wrecking it. This man has never failed—his plans have not been schemes to wreck and ruin. He is a builder of homes, a maker of genuine, lasting prosperity, an organizer who works for peace, beauty and all that makes for truth and excellence. Follow this man from St. Paul to Seattle and you will see permanent prosperity and smiling plenty have followed in his tread. Not only has he made money for himself, but he has made money for everyone in the Hill country who has been willing to take off his coat and get to work. James J. Hill, as a promoter of useful industry, stands alone, without a rival on earth. Like Pericles, he can truthfully say: "I have caused no one to wear crepe."

The Middle West supplied the conditions of growth, in which James J. Hill, Abraham Lincoln and Robert Ingersoll evolved.

One more name I wish to mention, and that is James Whitcomb Riley, who was evolved in the sunlight—product of the same soil—sung to by the same prairie winds.

We are a little too close to Riley to get the true perspective, and in some parts of America there be critics who yet mistake the simplicity and directness of Riley for things commonplace. He is an Æolean harp, and what these critics crave is a brass band. They prefer the speech of Spartacus to the Gladiators to the rhyme of the Raggedy Man. Let them have it.

In Riley's work there is a heart-welling quality—free from all bathos, the maudlin, the lachrymose and the hysterical that stamps the work as sublime. The man has wit, knows values, and he writes for himself and those he loves.

Riley is divinely human.

He is a product of sun and shadow, of summer clouds and winter winds, of cornfield, orchard and waving fields of ripening grain; of store, shop and factory, but I doubt me much if he would know a dactyl from an anapest, if he should see them coming down the street arm in arm. Riley sings because his heart sings.

It is heart that makes great art.

Riley has done classic work—it makes its appeal to the great throbbing impulses of humanity. We are all better because Riley writes. In his work there is no pretense, affectation and small trace of that which time lays hold upon and covers with verdigris. The man will live!

And the Middle West supplied the conditions of growth under

which he evolved.

Pretty good school that can turn out men like that?

Well, I should think so!

But—

The Conditions of Growth in America are yet far from perfect.

To be absolutely frank, we must admit that America has evolved a few other things beside great men. For instance, in all of our larger cities may be seen an occasional crescent-vested plute with two watch chains and a diamond dingus, who sends his boys to college because he has the money, and to get them out of the way, and because their Ma thinks it would be nice to have Josiah graduate at Harvard, for he would then lend reflected glory on her fetching Four-o'Clock.

What we must do as educators, is to ascertain as nearly as possible what the best conditions are, and then supply them.

Ed Geers said to me the other day, "We ruin ten thousand colts in order to produce one Lou Dillon."

It is much the same in society. Of all those who go down in darkness and defeat, trampled to their doom in the mad rush for place and power, we hear nothing.

We need the colleges, but not for segregation, nor yet for noisy yells and sophomoric pride in smug futility of Greek-letter societies, with their senseless, soulless mummery.

Why not a workshop instead?

The university of the future will supply certain conditions of growth and these will be free to all who care to work for them, and all who care to work for them will be free to do so.

If a man will not work, neither shall he eat.

If a man will not work, neither shall he be educated.

In future, our children shall go to school—not be sent nor sentenced. Nothing is of any value to you except what you work for. Things given you and thrust upon you are forever alien to you—separate and apart, and will be molted very shortly.

That which is worth having is worth working for.

Education is not an acquisition, it is an achievement. Like liberty, you must earn it, or you'll wander forever in the desert, a slave in spirit still. Love goes to those who are worthy, and education is the same. It takes work to secure an education; it takes work to use it, and it takes work to keep it.

Prove your worth by work!

The value of an education consists not in having gotten it, but in getting it.

LIFE LIES IN THE QUEST!

An Educated Person

The Philistine, January, 1904.

Not long ago a clergyman paid a visit to the fifth grade of a school, and was called upon to make a few remarks. This he did, enlarging on the beauty and excellence of being an educated person, and wound up by asking the scholars this question: "What is the difference between an educated and an uneducated man?"

This is a proposition too hard for grown-ups, but since children are always asking us questions we cannot answer, we give it back to them in kind, and thus get even.

"What is the difference between an educated and an uneducated man?"

Up went the hands.

"Well, you tell us, Mary," said the speaker to a nine-year-old girl with freckled face and a little mole on her chin. "An educated man is one who never does any work!" was the prompt and proud reply.

The clergyman himself told me the story. He was big enough to realize that this little child had unconsciously embodied in her answer a ringing, stinging truth—a reply worthy of Dean Swift, who never did a stroke of useful work in his life. "She hit me hard," said the man, "I am an educated person—at least I have degrees from two universities, and I do no useful thing. The sober truth is, the world could get along very well without me. I quit useful work to secure an education, and I have done nothing useful since. To be sure, I marry people; I christen children; I say things when they bury the dead; I make pastoral calls; I preach; I plan schemes for raising my salary. Now, children really do not require christening; people marry without me, and the best friend of the deceased at a funeral could do the task of saying the last words much more fittingly. The clergyman is a sociological appendenda, and the world of progress does not need us, nor does it need the seminaries, colleges and universities that unfit us for useful effort. But all this is for you, privately—promise me not to print it."

And I promised.

At Yale there are three thousand students, and twenty-seven hundred and forty-six of these students are remittance men. Send your boy to college and the remittance men will educate him.

In England and on the Continent it is worse. The ten thousand art students of Paris are remittance men. And they do not make artists, excepting as one in five thousand, like people who live down a consumptive taint. Jean-François Millet is the type that makes the artist.

Weary Willie and Cave-o'-the-Winds are possessed with the idea that the world owes them a living—and they go from house to house to collect it.

The typical educated person is full of the same thought—the world must feed and clothe him. If he is on half-rations, as he often is, he has a sad tale to tell of inappreciation and ingratitude. If the remittances continue through life, he is all right or fairly so. If the remittances are withdrawn, he becomes a public charge,—respectable possibly, but a public charge, just the same, for a tax is no less a tax because it is indirect.

The custom of schools and colleges supplying everything for the pupil, is a form of altruism that has its serious drawbacks. The biggest and best part of life lies in supplying yourself the things you need; and education, which is development, comes from doing without things, making things, and talking about things you do not have, a deal more than using things that rich men supply gratis.

If everything is done for us we will not do much for ourselves. If you knew of a school where your boy and girl, of sixteen to twenty, could go and earn a living while getting an education, would you not send them there?

I think you would—or you wouldn't, as the case may be.

To be able to earn a living is quite as necessary as to parse the Greek verb, a proposition which I trust needs no proof.

The reason the Industrial College has never been evolved, is because we have not, so far, evolved men big enough to captain both education and industry.

We have plenty of men big enough for college presidents—thousands of them. But we haven't men who can direct the energies of young men and women into useful channels, and at the same time feed their expanding minds. This is where we reach our limit, and reveal ourselves a race of pygmies. There is room for the man who can set in motion a curriculum that will embrace earning a living and mental growth, and have them move together hand in hand.

The task of the college president is not great—he doesn't have to show results. He is both judge and jury in trying his own case. He passes on the fitness of his output, and like Deity, he looks upon his work—and calls it good, and we take his word for it. And the great world of doers doesn't care whether it is good or not.

Note this: the grade teacher fits his pupils for the high school, and the high school teacher passes on the fitness of the grade teacher's product; the high school prepares the pupil for college, and the college teacher passes on the quality of the high school product; the college professor fits a pupil for life, and passes judgment on his own work. For him there is no censorship, and beyond him there is no appeal.

But life, which is greater than college, reviews the findings, and quietly ignores them all, just as we would disregard the injunction of a Justice of the Peace in North Carolina, who ordered that people in East

Aurora cease work on Tuesday. Life until yesterday, was considered one thing, and education another—which is exactly as it should not be.

For the man who can weld life and education, the laurel awaits.

The chief error of the colleges lies in the fact that they have separated the world of culture from the world of work. They have fostered the fallacy that one set of men should do the labor, and another set should have the education—that one should be ornamental and the other useful.

Then, to bolster their position, they have manufactured specious arguments trying to show that the professionals who supply truth and art to the poor people who have neither, are better than the folks who toil to feed and clothe the folks who make the arguments.

The fact is that the opportunities for education should be within the reach of every individual, not for the lucky few. Nature is opposed to monopolies and so she nips the selfish ambitions of your exclusively educated person and says, "Go to! get your education and be damned!"

And he often is.

Hence we get a condition approaching that which existed in the Fifteenth Century, when nobody was educated because the schools graduated only the top-heavy.

There is reason for congratulation in the fact that the first earnest protest against sequestering the student, in order to educate him, came from a college man, thus relieving the argument from the charge of "sour grapes." In 1865, John Ruskin wrote, "The methods in all of our colleges and most of our schools hark back to a time when education was designed alone for those who were to become priests. The student was regarded as one set apart, of the Order of Melchizedek."

In 1880, William Morris, the best pupil of John Ruskin, and himself an Oxford man, said, "We no longer believe in a class that is called, or set apart. Every man has a divine call to make himself useful to his fellows, and the hallucination that some are called to do nothing but give advice, will soon fade away. Industrial education is both moral and spiritual. The man who fails to use his body every day in a certain amount of manual labor is a menace to the State, and a danger to his inmost self. Safety lies in a just balance between head and hand."

To show how hopeful is our cause, tokening as it does that reform will come from within, I quote President Eliot, who recently said in a speech before the Independent Club of Buffalo, "I will never be satisfied until one-half the curriculum at Harvard is devoted to doing things, instead of merely talking about them." The preacher who is separated by education and custom from the world of useful effort, hasn't anything worth telling on Sunday. He cudgels his brain all the week to produce a terracotta dog to protect a make-believe teepee. He is like the convicts in the Elmira Reformatory, who build brick buildings and beautiful houses, and then take them all apart at the end of the week, so another gang can begin anew. Their hearts are not in their work—it is all pretense, and they never for a moment forget it.

The best way to learn to be useful is to be useful. To take a young man from life for four years and send him to college, in order to educate him for life is to run a grave risk that you will not get him back into life. The colleges are constantly graduating incompetent people, and this will continue until men get a living and an education at the same time.

To do no useful work for four years, in order that you may thereafter be useful, will someday be looked back upon as a barbaric blunder; like the Chinese method of curing epilepsy by rattling the dried seeds in a gourd.

A zealous graduate of Harvard has recently left twenty thousand dollars to his Alma Mater to build an iron fence around the college grounds. This fence is now in position, and is worth inspection. It is twelve feet high, with sharp iron spikes on top and brick buttresses eight feet square placed at short distances. It is horse-high, bull-strong and pig-tight. It will withstand a siege, and is as formidable as the walls about the Celestial City in Pekin, where Christians wither if they look therein. Fences are for three purposes—to keep things out, to keep things in, and for ornament, and ornament is for symbol.

Why a fence around Harvard? I'll tell you, it is to keep every creature that wears petticoats from getting inside and finding there is nothing there. That fence wasn't really built there at all. It is a secretion, and was evolved through desire, just as a porcupine secretes its quills. And if you know your Darwin, you will remember this, "The quills of a porcupine are to protect weakness—the raccoon, badger and ferret do not need them."

Over one of the gates at Harvard is this quotation, "If ye would know wisdom enter here." This makes one think of that sarcastic remark of St. Paul's, "If a woman would have wisdom, let her ask her husband." The march of progress will yet decree that every forbidding spike of Harvard's fence shall be turned into a pruning-hook, and its bars be beaten into plowshares.

That formidable fence symbols the popular idea of culture. It is exclusive. The common herd must not enter. The high fence is forbidding—there is no welcome in it—it means, stand back! Begone! Culture costs, and is for the elect few.

The truth is, college only supplies a few opportunities—books, lectures, association with other men. There is nothing wonderful about a college professor except his density. He perhaps knows his specialty, but outside of this he is apt to be a very lop-sided person. One advantage of the big college is that students do not usually get personally acquainted with their teachers. The association of students with students is often regarded as a great advantage, and we hear much of "friction of mind." But when we remember that for the most part, college students are absolutely exempt from useful effort, there is a grave question as to the value of association, being as it is, the association of idle men.

In all of the large cities of America there are University Clubs, to which no man is eligible as a member, nor welcome as a visitor, unless he has a university degree. No one nowadays has the hardihood to claim that a degree is proof of power, but we see that men become exclusive, and band themselves together on account of the pride they possess in having done a thing which possibly, was merely vacuous and fatuous, like unto a man keeping three balls in the air, and balancing a feather on his nose at the same time. As to physical culture in universities, it is always optional, and is mostly limited to the athletes, that is to say, to those who need it least.

I tack the following theses on every college bulletin-board, and every church door in Christendom, and stand ready to publicly debate and defend them, six nights and days together, 'gainst all comers— college presidents and preachers preferred.

1.—Man's education is never complete, and life and education should go hand in hand to the end.

2.—By separating education from practical life society has inculcated the vicious belief that education is one thing and life another.

3.—Five hours of intelligently directed work a day will supply ample board, lodging and clothing to the adolescent student, male or female.

4.—Five hours of manual labor will not only support the student, but it will add to his intellectual vigor and conduce to his better physical, mental and spiritual development.

5.—This work should be directly in the line of education, and a part of the school curriculum.

6.—No effort of life need be inutile, but all effort should be useful in order to satisfy the consciousness.

7.—Somebody must do the work of the world. There is a certain amount of work to do, and the reason some people have to labor from daylight until dark is because others never work at all.

8.—To do a certain amount of manual labor every day, should be accounted a privilege to every normal man and woman.

9.—No person should be overworked.

10.—All should do some work.

11.—To work intelligently is education.

12.—To abstain from useful work in order to get an education, is to get an education of the wrong kind, that is to say, a false education.

13.—From fourteen years up, every normal individual can be self-supporting, and to be so is a God-given privilege, conducive to the best mental, moral and spiritual development.

14.—The plan of examinations, in order to ascertain how much the pupil knows, does not reveal how much the pupil knows, causes much misery, is conducive to hypocrisy, and is like pulling up the plant to examine its roots. It further indicates that we have small faith in our methods.

15.—People who have too much leisure, consume more than they should, and do not produce enough.

16.—To go to school for four years, or six, is no proof of excellence; any more than to fail in an examination is proof of incompetence.

17.—The giving of degrees and diplomas to people who have done no useful things is puerile and absurd, since degrees so secured are no proof of competence, and tend to inflate the holder with the idea that he is some great one when, probably, he isn't.

18.—All degrees should be honorary, and be given for meritorious service to society—that is, for doing something useful for somebody.

19.—The walls of the old-time college are crumbling, and the University of the future will have around it no twelve-foot-high iron fence.

What is a Genius?

The Philistine, June, 1903.

I never saw a genius, and really do not know what a genius is, but surely there is plenty of precedent for speaking upon themes concerning which we know nothing. Goodness me!

But my idea is that a genius is a man who has the faculty of doing certain excellent things in a masterly way. What other men work out with sweat and lamp-smoke this man does jauntily, joyously, and without seeming thought or effort. While others are talking about the thing, he does it. And he can never tell how or why.

No dictionary can define this faculty of genius.

No chemist can analyze it.

It seems to be a flash of the divine spark that goes straight to the heart of things.

The man simply sees—that is all. And seeing he says, or writes, or acts.

And depend upon this: direct and forceful doing is always the result of direct and vivid seeing. When you write luminously, without fog or mist, it is because there is no fog in your brain. Before you can make others see the picture you must first see it yourself.

All those explanations about genius being "the ability to concentrate," and "the capacity for hard work," are clever but fallacious. You may have "the ability to concentrate" and "the capacity for hard work" and yet be mediocre. To be sure, the genius has the ability to concentrate, but he has something more. Some of us who have tuppence worth of talent can conserve it, and by judicious exercise and tutoring grow to a point where we do fairly good work. But where is the professor of literature who could have shown Shakespeare how to write "Hamlet," or the art school that could have instructed Michelangelo how to fresco the Chapel of Sixtus, or the painter who could have mixed the colors for Turner's "Carthage," or the pedagog who could have instructed Edison in physics?

Yet we know nothing is done by chance. The miraculous is the natural not yet understood—there are laws that regulate this supreme flash of the intellect. But all we know is that at long intervals we see its manifestation. Genius seems to be a sample of God's power, sent just to show us the possible. If one man out of a million may be supremely wise and efficient for a little while, why may he not in time be wise and efficient all the time? And what one man may attain, why may not the race attain?

Emerson says, "A man is a god in ruins." This seems to imply that man is a failure, but the real fact is, Emerson, in this instance, has reversed the truth. A baby is no failure, even if it can do nothing but eat, sleep, coo and cry—and surely we can love the baby.

A man is a god in the crib.

Now the genius is only a genius a part of the time. His moments of insight are transient, and there may be days or weeks or months that are fallow. Then comes a quick gathering up of forces and a glory stands revealed for which the man had been groping for years.

Corot, catching the sunlight on his palette and transferring it to canvas, was once so surprised and gladdened that he burst into song, and shouted for joy. And wishing to share his joy with another he looked about, and saw a peasant trudging along the road. Corot ran to him, embraced the astonished man, and seizing him by the arm, ran him across the meadow, and standing him before the canvas, said, "Look at that! Look at that! I've got it at last—look at that!"

The peasant didn't see it—he hadn't been looking for it—and the sunlight not being in his soul, he could not perceive it when it was mirrored in a picture.

No, the peasant didn't see it, but he saw a "wild look" in Corot's eyes, and making haste to disengage himself, went home and told his wife that the painter-man was crazy.

But Corot wasn't crazy. He was as sane to the last as Walt Whitman.

The fact that one man sees things the average man cannot, and knows things the average man does not, is no proof of insanity—hardly, brother!

Corot wasn't crazy—he merely seemed crazy.

"This man hath a devil and is mad"—but he wasn't, that was only the opinion of certain people.

Men of supreme intellect do not go insane—it is lack of intellect that makes most of the trouble. And so the opposite of things always seems alike. When Shakespeare said, "Great genius is to madness near allied," he knew better. He was just passing out a popular fallacy to tickle the ears of the groundlings. But this little extension of mental power which we call genius, has ever gotten its owners into trouble. People cannot comprehend it, and so they resent it. It is an insult—the man does not conform—he goes his own gait—he forgets the things that to others are vital: cards, curds and custards are nothing to him. He sees God in the burning bush and wants to ask Him a question.

Read the history of Beethoven, Michelangelo, Leonardo, Shakespeare, Shelley, Byron, and you read a tale of family and domestic woe.

The genius is a sore trial. Even Jesus was not exempt: His mother and brethren saw the extravagance of His acts, and wished to take Him back in safety to their country home. And He, wearied with their importunities, once for a moment lost His poise, and with a touch of impatience said to His mother, "Woman, what have I to do with thee!"

Should a genius marry, let him follow the example of Goethe, who used to refer to his wife as "a convenient loaf of brown bread." Of course, the ideal would be to find a woman whose mind matches his own—who knows his worth and sympathizes with his ideals—and here our memory runs straight to the Brownings.

But the chances are that the genius neither takes to himself the loaf of brown bread nor does he find his Elizabeth Barrett. And being a genius only at intervals, and the rest of the time an average man, he marries an average woman. Opinions, as usual, are divided as to whether the man is a genius or a fool. His kinsmen, who have known him from childhood, say he is a fool or a rogue—his conduct to them is always an affront. The wife wishes to keep on good terms with her kinsmen and with society, and still she wishes to be loyal to her husband. She wishes to help him—to be his inspiration. The pace is too rapid—the woman grows breathless from running, and seeks to hold the man back. He tries to carry her, but soon finds he cannot. She wishes to minister to his "higher nature," but how can she when he seems to want nothing but to be let alone!

She weeps.

Her dissatisfaction is with herself, but this she does not know.

We lay blame elsewhere, and take all credit to ourselves.

The great outside world of men and women does not know the man excepting by his work. They see his picture, his statue, his book, or they listen to his oration, his song, or watch his performance from the parquet. He gives to the public his best, and the public breaks into applause. They demand his autograph, his photograph, they want the honor of shaking hands with him. His wife is pointed out as a mere appendage—nobody cares for her! She is wrung and stung—is she a stock, a stone, a slave, a thing? Ah! she will show them! Straightway she sets out to be clever, too. She seeks to rival her liege and turn the current of admiration her way. She writes a book, or prepares a "paper," or sings in public, or "recites," or displays her beauty in unique and splendid gowns. But alas! the letters still come demanding her husband's autograph, women stare at her coldly—it is all for him! She is powerless against his genius, and so is he.

Chills of fear and fevers of heat chase each other across the soul. The public does not know her husband! It sees only the one side. She knows him—yes, I guess so. He deceives the public into the belief that he is some great one! The words of unkind criticism and vituperation that she occasionally sees in the newspapers please her. The kinsmen are right—the man is a fakir, a fraud, a poseur, a pretender—she knows—I guess so!

He uses a toothbrush, and the manicure set she bought him Christmas—or he doesn't. He stands before the mirror shaving and makes horrible grimaces. He talks to himself—goes to walk, and forgets lunchtime. Company comes to see her, and he sits at the table stupid. And still the fools write for his autograph, and the lunatics ask for his photograph.

She weeps.

He no longer loves her—he goes to the woods alone. He does not tell her his plans. He declines to go to receptions or fetes—he writes or works half the night.

She now demands attention as her due—asserts her rights, and boldly affronts the autograph fiends and bids the fools who come on pious pilgrimages, begone.

She mistakes her husband's abstraction for stupidity, and seeks to rail him into a better way of life. She chides, rebukes, and—he awakening out of his lethargy, proves his common clay by railing back.

Alas! It confirms her suspicions—he is only clay and common clay at that.

To show him how it is, himself, she now has company of her own—floorwalkers, clerks from the ribbon counter, players on the clarionet, tenors who sing in amateur operas.

When a man ceases to pay court to his wife, other men are apt to. These callers are smart in attire, smart in repartee, clever, attentive. They are like the suitors in the house of Ulysses—they overrun the place.

But not eternally—for one fine day a tenor being too smart, laboring under the popular illusion that the genius is a fool, finds himself kicked into the street, and a clarionet (through error) tossed after him. There are feminine tears, protests in contralto, threats,—and now surely the man is no genius: he is simply a plain brute: a wife-beater—or nearly so.

She weeps.

She is losing her husband—he is no longer wholly hers—he is slipping away, away.

Their house is no longer a home—it is only an office or a studio.

She begins a system of espionage—letters are opened—duplicate keys play their part—servants are taken into her confidence. And her punishment consists in finding her suspicions true.

We find that for which we seek. "That which I feared has come upon me." The thing we fear we bring to pass.

And now the heart that should be filled with tenderness and gentle mother-love becomes an abyss of cruelty and revenge. She is willing, aye, anxious to disgrace, destroy and damn to lowest hell that which she once worshipped as divine.

Jealousy and murder are only a step apart.

"The man is to blame," you say. And you are right. His offense lies in his power, against which he is powerless. If he had not the power to express, to do, to influence, to mold, to attract, he would never have given offense to this woman or anyone else. He is to blame; but yet he is blameless because he is what he is. And she is blameless for the same reason.

We sympathize with him; but her—we pity.

The artist is always selfish—he sacrifices everybody and everything in order to get the work done. Cellini casting his "Perseus" and throwing into the molten mass all of the family plate in order to get the statue complete, reveals the man. Palissy burning up the furniture in order to bring the furnace to the proper degree of heat, is the true type.

The artist is selfish,—yes, supremely selfish.

And here is my advice to all women who are married to men who love their work better than they love their wives: Do not nag, do not struggle, do not obstruct, do not fight, do not rival—just be yourself. You are only lovable when you are yourself. Be a nobody, and sink yourself in your work, just as your husband sinks himself in his work.

If your husband is great, he is great on account of his work—that is his virtue. He knows this, and his admiration is for the person who does his work.

And in useful work, at the last, there is no degree. It is all necessary, and the woman told of by Theodore Parker, who swept the room to the glory of God, deserves and shall have her crown.

Just here I feel like apologizing for having referred to a woman— any woman—as "a convenient loaf of brown bread." It was Goethe's expression, and not mine. I have too much respect for womanhood to speak lightly of women. The best that is in my soul has been absorbed from women. So I would rather put a new construction on Goethe's simile and say there is nothing more nutritious, nothing more useful, nothing so satisfying as brown bread.

Please pass the brown bread.

If you are a loaf of brown bread, thank God, but do not pretend you are a frosted cake, or a plum pudding. You will surely disappoint somebody, and there will be for you a day of reckoning.

When the Paris mob assailed the palace at Versailles crying for bread, and Marie Antoinette in her innocence asked, "Why don't they eat cake?" she revealed a gastronomic fallacy—cake as a steady diet is not advisable. Please pass the brown bread. The clerk at the ribbon counter may be won by frosted cake with frills, sprinkled with red-sanded sugar and caraway seed, but not so the man of power. He wants brown bread.

And at last the woman who can sink her oriental instinct and be willing to be a somebody and do her work and sweep her room to the glory of God, completes the circle and reveals the great and splendid personality. By giving all, she shall win all. Simple honesty, simple integrity—no secrets, no schemes.

And from my limited experience in these matters I gather that the plain and unpretentious woman often has a splendid mind, and a deal of sturdy common sense, and is very much more likely to appreciate her husband's genius, and make allowance for his limitations, than a wife who runs rival to her lord and has a furtive eye on fame for herself.

Be a woman, a plain honest woman—the mother of men—and the man of power will go to you and lay his tired head in your lap, and with tears of gratitude, bless the Giver of all Good that you are his, that you minister to him, cheer him on his way, nourish and refresh him—that you are a loaf of brown bread, and not a ginger cookie upon which mice and tenors nibble.

Please pass the brown bread.

Maeterlinck in writing of the bees asks, "Why do they thus renounce sleep, the delights of honey and love, and exquisite leisure enjoyed, for instance, by their winged brothers, the butterfly? Two or three flowers suffice for their nourishment, yet in an hour they will visit two hundred in order to collect a treasure which they will never taste. Why all this toil and distress, and whence this mighty assurance that all is well? Is it so certain then that the new generation whereunto you offer your lives will merit the sacrifice; will be more beautiful, happier, will do something you have not done because you have thus toiled?"

And the bees do not answer. Neither does the genius know why he thus works, and dares, and does, and offers himself and his all for a good that is yet unborn.

He does not know—he lives by faith. And of the Power that guides his footsteps and leads him on, he knows nothing more than does the bee. Continually he hears the Voice, "Arise and get thee hence, for this is not thy rest." And through snow and ice, through dust and heat, through glaring day and darkest night his answer to the Voice is ever instant and implicit obedience. The spirit of abnegation that gives all, and thereby wins all, is upon him: "Lord here am I!" And this abnegation—this obedience that neither stands, nor sits, nor hesitates, but goes, is the price of achievement.

Advantages and Disadvantages

The Philistine, January, 1901.

The so-called "disadvantages" in the life of a child are often its advantages. And on the other hand, "advantages" are often disadvantages of a most serious sort. To be born in the country, of poor parents, is no disadvantage. The strong men in every American city— the men who can do things; the men like James J. Hill, Charles E. Perkins, Philip G. Armour, Norton G. Finney, C. C. Merrill, or the late Tom Potter, who gloried in difficulties, waxed strong in overcoming obstacles, and laughed at disaster—men who could build three miles of railroad a day, and cause prosperous cities to spring up where before were only swamps and jungle, barren plains or endless forest—these men were all country boys, nurtured in adversity.

And it is but the tritest truism to say that the early life of industry, and unceasing economy of time and things, was the best possible preparation and education that these men could have had for doing a great work.

I once heard George M. Pullman tell how, at ten years of age, he used to cut wood so his mother could cook, help her wash the dishes and sweep; carry water for her to do the washing, and assist her hanging out the clothes. In a year or two more he planted the garden, knew all kinds of vegetable seeds on sight, knew every forest tree that grew in Western New York and could distinguish between the qualities of the wood. At seventeen he helped his father move houses and barns and dig wells and construct church steeples. That is to say he was getting an education—learning to do things in the best way. He was developing physique, and also building character and making soul-fiber. He was learning to make plans and execute them, think for himself and be strong and self-reliant. Yet he didn't know it at the time, and later regretted his lack of education and absence of opportunity.

Pullman was always a little too busy to be a philosopher; in spite of his mighty grasp on practical things he failed to perceive that he was a product of the "unkind conditions" of his boyhood. He plumed himself on overcoming great difficulties; in after-dinner confidences occasionally recited the great things he had done and compared them to the still greater things he might have done "if he had only had a chance."

Perhaps George M. Pullman knew down deep in his heart that he had received the very best training possible for his life-work; but that quality in "self-made" men which causes them to want all the credit for the job, blinded him to a great degree to the truth. Hence we find him protecting his own sons from the blessings that had been his. Instead of having his boys brought up to do things, he had servants who cheated them out of all that round of daily duties which had made him strong. He had tutors who taught them things out of books and gave them advice. The result was that the sons of George M. Pullman are pretty nearly moral defectives and their fantastic tricks before high heaven have added to the gaiety of nations. Someone has said, "You know what God thinks of millionaires when you see the kind of men he gives the money to."

Pullman's boys are without even a trace of that decision and strength that made their father famous. George M. Pullman could operate a great industry but he could not bring up a family. He succeeded in everything but the boy business.

The method pursued by George M. Pullman in educating his boys is the plan pursued by most rich men. All that they gain for the world is lost again in their children.

And until yesterday all the college presidents and all the pedagogs who lectured and taught and wrote and preached, fully endorsed the plan adopted by George M. Pullman in educating his boys.

So sternly true is this that Dr. Edward Everett Hale, a graduate of Harvard, has said, "If you should take twelve prize medal men from Harvard and put them on a sinking ship they would all drown through inability to construct a raft."

The mote-blind pedagogs are quite willing to keep on stuffing boys with impressions, not knowing that the number of impressions a boy can hold is limited. We grow through expression, and the large colleges, even yet, afford a very imperfect means for expression—all is impression and repression. But today we find a few of the highest type of teachers making a bold stand for the natural method of education. That is, they recognize that the education which George M. Pullman received was a better, wiser and safer education than the education which George M. Pullman gave to his boys. Last week I visited the John Dewey School of Chicago and there I saw them doing for the children, with carefully prepared intent, just what fate, poverty and "unkind conditions" did for George M. Pullman.

John Dewey, the head of the Dewey School, is a pupil of that noted psychologist and thoroughly sane man, Dr. Stanley Hall, and the cry of Dr. Hall is, "Back to Nature."

At the Dewey School they try to teach children just as a kind, intelligent and loving mother would teach her children if she lived away off forty miles from nowhere, and had an income of three hundred dollars a year to support a family of nine.

Nothing interests us save as it comes home to us as a personal issue. And in visiting the Dewey School I unconsciously compared it with my own early lack of instruction.

When I was fifteen years of age I could break wild horses to saddle or harness, and teach kicking cows to stand while they were being milked. I could fell trees and drop the tree in any direction desired; I knew the relative value of all native woods; appreciated the difference in soil, grains, fruits and simple minerals. I could use the drawshave, adz, axe, broadaxe, crosscut saw, sickle and cradle. I could make a figure-four trap, an axe helve, a neckyoke, oxyoke, whiffle-trees, clevis, and braid an eight-strand cattle whip. We used to mend our harness on rainy days and I could make a wax-end and thread it with a bristle, and use a bradawl. I knew how to construct an ash-leach and to make soft soap, apple butter and pumpkin pies. I knew the process of weaving flax and wool, of making and burning brick. I knew on sight and had names for a score or more of birds, and had a good idea of the habits of squirrels, skunks, wolves and the fishes that swam in the creeks. I knew how to cure hams, shoulders and sidemeat; to pickle beef, and cover apples with straw and earth so they would keep in safety through the most severe winter and open up in the spring, fresh and valuable.

Of course my knowledge was not of scientific order, and I could not have explained it to another, because I never knew I had it. It all came along easily, naturally and as a matter of course. It would be absurd to say that I was an expert worker in all the lines I have mentioned, but I was familiar with the processes and could do things with my hands all in my own crude way, just as I daily saw my father and the neighbors do.

And so when I saw at this experimental school of the Chicago University, the same curriculum being worked out that I had known in youth, I could not but smile. Prof. John Dewey with his costly apparatus and heavy endowment, is merely trying to overcome the "advantages of civilization."

They have no wild horses nor kicking cows in the Dewey School, but they teach children to make things out of wood, iron and cloth. They are taught to measure, weigh and compare and decide. They wash dishes and put things away in a neat and orderly manner. They are taught the nature of wool, cotton and flax, and are shown how to weave, dye and construct. They learn without knowing when or how they learn. The repression and discipline that one feels in many schools is removed and there is an air of freedom in the place that is very helpful. It's a curious experiment—this back to nature—but in the line of truth.

The success of an individual is usually damnation for his children. Luxury enervates and kills, and this is the reason that the race has made such slow and painful progress. All one generation gains is lost in the next. The great nations have died from off the earth simply because they succeeded. The grandeur that was Greece and the glory that was Rome, are but names writ in water. The splendours of Spain and Italy are crumbling into dust. Whether France and England have not expressed their best is a question—nations, like families, die the death and they die because they win.

Institutions similar to the Dewey School are attempts to hold the ground once gained, and as such they should command the earnest consideration and respect of every man who knows history and who realizes that the progress of civilization has been only a repetition of the labor of Sisyphus.

We grow strong through doing things. And when one generation comes into possession of the material good that the former generation has gained, and makes that fool remark, "I don't have to work," it straightway is stepping on the chute that gives it a slide to Avernus—and then all has to be done over again.

I expect to see the day when schoolteachers will not be supplied a beautiful scarcity of everything but hard work. I expect to see the day when no schoolteacher will have more than twenty pupils.

I expect to see the day when the honors and compensation of school teaching will command the services of the strongest and best men and women in every community.

I expect to see the day when the conversational method will be supreme, and teaching will be done practically without books,—by object lessons, thinking things out and doing things.

I expect to see the day when overwrought nerves in teacher or pupil will be unknown, for joy will take the place of anxiety, and all the bugaboo of examinations will be consigned to limbo. The evolution even now is at work, and the time is ripe. The beauty seen in all schoolrooms, and the reaching out for harmony are not in vain. These things are bearing fruit.

This is the richest country the world has ever known. We are loaning money to Europe—and ideas, too. We spend a sum total in America of two hundred million dollars a year for the support of our public schools. Yet we raised a like sum recently for war and fighting machines, and no one lifted an eyebrow, except a few cranks around Boston and a man in Nebraska.

Now suppose that we awake to the truth that war is waste, and worse,—that we stand in no danger and need few soldiers, and that we would better educate our boys and girls at home than indulge in doubtful Old World experiments—then what! Why, we'll reduce our fighting force and use the money to increase the efficiency of our teaching force. We will let children grow strong and unfold through doing things and talking about them as they do them, and pupils and teacher will grow strong together. We will do away with truancy, trampism, hoodlumism and lessen crime by nine-tenths. We will not suppress bad or restless boys, we will divert them and direct their energies into paths of usefulness.

And the day is coming.

For these thoughts are not my thoughts. They are in the hearts of thousands in every city, town, hamlet and village—east or west, north or south—it's just God's truth. And when enough people arrive at truth, and realize that every day is judgment day and the important place is here, and the time is now, then we will work for a present good, and educate, not kill; love, not hate; and the men and women who educate most and best, shall be honored most. The day is dawning in the East.

Remember the Week-Day to Keep it Holy

The Philistine, November, 1903.

I am not so sure about this, Blessed, but if I am wrong you will please put me straight: it is an absurd and semi-barbaric thing to set one day apart as "holy."

If you are a writer, and a beautiful thought comes to you, you never hesitate because it is Sunday—you write it down.

If you are a painter, and the picture appears before you, vivid and clear, you make haste to materialize it ere the vision fades.

If you are a musician, you sing a song, or play it on the piano, that it may be etched upon your memory—and for the joy of it.

But if you are a cabinet-maker, you may make the design, but you will halt before making the table, if the day be the "Lord's Day;" and if you are a blacksmith, you will not lift a hammer, for fear of conscience or the police. All of which is an admission that manual labor is a sort of necessary evil, and must be done at certain times and places, as cesspools are emptied at night.

The idea of serving God on Sunday and forgetting Him all the week is a fallacy fostered by the Rev. Dr. Sayles and his coadjutor, Deacon Buffum, who passes the Panama for the benefit of those who would buy absolution. Or, if you prefer, salvation being free, what we place in the Panama is an honorarium for Deity or His Agent, just as noted authors never speak at banquets for pay, but accept the honorarium that is mysteriously placed on the mantel.

Sunday, with its immunity from work, was devised for slaves who got out of all the work they could during the week.

Then, to tickle the approbativeness of the slave, it was declared a virtue not to work on Sunday, a most pleasing bit of Tom Sawyer diplomacy. By following his inclinations and doing nothing, a mysterious, skyey benefit accrues, in which the lazy man hopes to participate.

Then the slaves who do not work on Sunday point out those who do as beneath them in virtue and deserving of contempt. Upon this theory all laws punishing the person who works or plays on Sundays have been passed.

Does God cease work one day in seven, or is the work He does on Sunday especially different from that which He performs on Tuesday?

The Saturday half-holiday is not "sacred"—the Sunday holiday is.

No man can violate the Sabbath; he can, however, violate his own nature, and this he is more apt to do through enforced idleness than in either work or play. Only running water is pure, and stagnant nature of any sort is dangerous—a breeding-place for disease.

Change of occupation is necessary to mental and physical health. As it is, most people get too much of one kind of work. All the week they are chained to a task, a repugnant task because the dose is too big. They have to do this particular job or starve. This is slavery, quite as much as when man was sold as a chattel.

Will not there come a time when all men and women will work because it is a blessed privilege? Then, if all worked, wasteful consuming as a business would cease. As it is, there are many people who do not work at all, and these pride themselves on it and uphold the Sunday laws. If the idlers would work, nobody would be overworked. If this time ever comes shall we not cease to regard it as "wicked" to work at certain times, just as much as we should count it absurd to pass a law making it illegal to be happy on Thursday? Isn't good work an effort to produce a useful, necessary, or beautiful thing?

If so, good work is a prayer, prompted by a loving heart—a prayer to benefit and bless.

If prayer isn't a desire, backed up by a right human effort to bring about its efficacy, then what is it?

Work is a service performed for ourselves and others. If I love you, I surely will work for you—in this way I reveal my love. And thus to make manifest my love is a joy and gratification for me. Thus work is for the worker.

These things being true, if it is wrong to work on Sunday it is wrong to love on Sunday: every smile is a sin, every caress a curse, and all tenderness crime.

Must there not come a time, if we grow in mentality and in spirit, when we shall cease to differentiate and quit calling some work secular and some sacred? Isn't it as necessary for me to hoe corn to feed my loved ones (and also the priest) as for the priest to preach and pray? Would any priest every preach or pray if somebody didn't hoe. If life is from God, then all useful effort is divine; and to work is the highest form of religion. If God made us, surely He is pleased to see that His work is a success. If we are miserable, willing to liberate life with a bare bodkin, we certainly do not compliment our Maker in thus regarding His work as a failure. But if our lives are full of gladness and we are grateful for the consciousness that we are one with Deity—helping God to do His work, then, and only then do we truly serve Him.

Isn't it strange that men should ever have made laws declaring it wicked to work?

Get Out or Get in Line

The Cosmopolitan, April, 1902.

If all the letters, messages and speeches of Lincoln were destroyed, except that one letter to Hooker, we should have a good index to the heart of the Rail-Splitter.

In this letter we see that Lincoln ruled his own spirit; and we also behold the fact that he could rule others. The letter shows frankness, kindliness, wit, tact, wise diplomacy and infinite patience.

Hooker had harshly and unjustly criticized Lincoln, his Commander-in-Chief, and he had embarrassed Burnside, his ranking officer. But Lincoln waives all this in deference to the virtues that he believes Hooker possesses, and promotes him to succeed Burnside. In other words, the man who had been wronged promotes the man who had wronged him, over the head of a man whom the promotee had wronged and for whom the promoter had a warm personal friendship.

But all personal considerations were sunk in view of the end desired. Yet it was necessary that the man promoted should know the truth, and Lincoln told it to him in a way that did not humiliate nor fire to foolish anger; but which certainly prevented the attack of cerebral elephantiasis to which Hooker was liable.

Perhaps we had better give the letter entire, and so here it is:

EXECUTIVE MANSION,
WASHINGTON, January 26, 1863.

MAJOR-GENERAL HOOKER:

GENERAL: I have placed you at the head of the Army of the Potomac. Of course, I have done this upon what appear to me to be sufficient reasons, and yet I think it best for you to know that there are some things in regard to which I am not quite satisfied with you.

I believe you to be a brave and skilful soldier, which, of course, I like.

I also believe you do not mix politics with your profession, in which you are right.

You have confidence in yourself, which is a valuable if not indispensable quality.

You are ambitious, which, within reasonable bounds, does good rather than harm, but I think that during General Burnside's command of the army you have taken counsel of your ambition and thwarted him as much as you could, in which you did a great wrong to the country and to a most meritorious and honorable brother officer.

I have heard, in such a way as to believe it, of your recently saying that both the army and the government needed a dictator. Of course, it was not for this, but in spite of it, that I have given you the command. Only those generals who gain successes can set up dictators. What I now ask of you is military success, and I will risk the dictatorship. The government will support you to the utmost of its ability, which is neither more nor less than it has done and will do for all commanders. I much fear that the spirit you have aided to infuse into the army, of criticizing their commander and with- holding confidence from him, will now turn upon you. I shall assist you as far as I can to put it down. Neither you nor Napoleon, if he were alive again, could get any good out of an army while such a spirit prevails in it. And now, beware of rashness; beware of rashness, but with energy and sleepless vigilance go forward and give us victories.

Yours, very truly,

A. LINCOLN.

One point in this letter is especially worth our consideration, for it suggests a condition that springs up like deadly nightshade from a poisonous soil. I refer to the habit of sneering, carping, grumbling at and criticizing those who are above us. The man who is anybody and who does anything is surely going to be criticized, vilified and misunderstood. This is a part of the penalty for greatness, and every great man understands it; and understands, too, that it is no proof of greatness. The final proof of greatness lies in being able to endure contumely without resentment. Lincoln did not resent criticism; he knew that every life must be its own excuse for being, but look how he calls Hooker's attention to the fact that the dissension Hooker has sown is going to return and plague him! "Neither you nor Napoleon, were he alive, could get any good out of an army while such a spirit prevails in it." Hooker's fault falls on Hooker—others suffer, but Hooker suffers most of all.

Not long ago I met a Yale student, home on a vacation. I am sure he did not represent the true Yale spirit, for he was full of criticism and bitterness toward the institution. President Hadley came in for his share, and I was supplied items, facts, data, with times and places, for a "peach of a roast."

Very soon I saw the trouble was not with Yale, the trouble was with the young man. He had mentally dwelt on some trivial slights until he had got so out of harmony with the institution that he had lost the power to derive any benefit from it. Yale is not a perfect institution—a fact, I suppose, that President Hadley and most Yale men are quite willing to admit; but Yale does supply certain advantages, and it depends upon the students whether they will avail themselves of these advantages or not.

If you are a student in a college, seize upon the good that is there.

You get good by giving it. You gain by giving—so give sympathy and cheerful loyalty to the institution. Be proud of it. Stand by your teachers—they are doing the best they can. If the place is faulty, make it a better place by an example of cheerfully doing your work every day the best you can. Mind your own business.

If the concern where you are employed is all wrong, and the Old Man a curmudgeon, it may be well for you to go to the Old Man and confidentially, quietly and kindly tell him that he is a curmudgeon. Explain to him that his policy is absurd and preposterous. Then show him how to reform his ways, and you might offer to take charge of the concern and cleanse it of its secret faults.

Do this, or if for any reason you should prefer not, then take your choice of these: Get Out or Get in Line. You have got to do one or the other—now make your choice.

If you work for a man, in heaven's name work for him!

If he pays you wages that supply you your bread and butter, work for him—speak well of him, think well of him, stand by him and stand by the institution he represents.

I think if I worked for a man I would work for him. I would not work for him a part of the time, and the rest of the time work against him. I would give an undivided service or none.

If put to the pinch, an ounce of loyalty is worth a pound of cleverness.

If you must vilify, condemn and eternally disparage, why, resign your position and, when you are outside, damn to your heart's content. But, I pray you, so long as you are a part of an institution, do not condemn it. Not that you will injure the institution—not that—but when you disparage the concern of which you are a part, you disparage yourself.

More than that, you are loosening the tendrils that hold you to the institution, and the first high wind that comes along, you will be uprooted and blown away in the blizzard's track—and probably you will never know why. The letter only says, "Times are dull and we regret there is not enough work," et cetera.

Everywhere you find those out-of-a-job fellows. Talk with them and you will find that they are full of railing, bitterness and condemnation. That was the trouble—through a spirit of fault-finding they got themselves swung around so they blocked the channel, and had to be dynamited. They are out of harmony with the concern, and no longer being a help they had to be removed. Every employer is constantly looking for people who can help him; naturally he is on the outlook among his employees for those who do not help, and everything and everybody that is a hindrance has to go. This is the law of trade—do not find fault with it; it is founded on Nature. The reward is only for the man that helps, and in order to help you must have sympathy.

You cannot help the Old Man so long as you are explaining in undertone and whisper, by gesture and suggestion, by thought and mental attitude, that he is a curmudgeon and his system dead wrong. You are not necessarily menacing him by stirring up discontent and warming envy into strife, but you are doing this: You are getting yourself upon a wellgreased chute that will give you a quick ride down and out.

When you say to other employees that the Old Man is a curmudgeon, you reveal the fact that you are one; and when you tell that the policy of the institution is "rotten," you surely show that yours is.

Hooker got his promotion even in spite of his failings: but the chances are that your employer does not have the love that Lincoln had—the love that suffereth long and is kind. But even Lincoln could not protect Hooker forever. Hooker failed to do the work, and Lincoln had to try someone else. So there came a time when Hooker was superseded by a Silent Man, who criticized no one, railed at nobody—not even the enemy. And this Silent Man, who ruled his own spirit, took the cities. He minded his own business, and did the work that no man ever can do unless he gives absolute loyalty, perfect confidence and untiring devotion.

Let us mind our own business, and work for self by working for the good of all.

Mental Attitude

Little Journeys to the Homes of English Authors, 1900.

Success is in the blood.

There are men whom Fate can never keep down—they march jauntily forward, and take by divine right the best of everything that earth affords. But their success is not attained by the Doctor Samuel Smiles Connecticut policy. They do not lie in wait, nor scheme, nor fawn, nor seek to adapt their sails to catch the breeze of popular favor. Still, they are ever alert and alive to any good that may come their way, and when it comes they simply appropriate it, and tarrying not, move steadily forward.

Good health! Whenever you go out of doors, draw the chin in, carry the crown of your head high, and fill the lungs to the utmost; drink in sunshine; greet your friends with a smile, and put soul into every hand-clasp. Do not fear being misunderstood and never waste a minute thinking about your enemies. Try to fix firmly in your mind what you would like to do, and then without violence of direction you will move straight to the goal.

Fear is the rock on which we split, and hate is the shoal on which many a bark is stranded. When we are fearful, the judgment is as unreliable as the compass of a ship whose hold is full of iron ore; when we hate, we have unshipped the rudder; and if we stop to meditate on what the gossips say, we have allowed a hawser to befoul the screw.

Keep your mind on the great and splendid thing you would like to do; and then, as the days go gliding by, you will find yourself unconsciously seizing upon the opportunities that are required for the fulfilment of your desire, just as the coral-insect takes from the running tide the elements that it needs. Picture in your mind the able, earnest, useful person you desire to be, and the thought you hold is hourly transforming you into that particular individual. Thought is supreme, and to think is often better than to do.

Preserve a right mental attitude—the attitude of courage, frankness and good-cheer.

To think rightly is to create.

Darwin and Spencer have told us that this is the method of Creation. Each animal has evolved the parts it needed and desired. The horse is fleet because it wishes to be; the bird flies because it desires to; the duck has a web-foot because it wants to swim. All things come through desire, and every sincere prayer is answered. Many people know this, but they do not believe it thoroughly enough so that it shapes their lives.

We want friends, so we scheme and chase 'cross lots after strong people, and lie in wait for good folks—or alleged good folks—hoping to attach ourselves to them. The only way to secure friends is to be one.

And before you are fit for friendship you must be able to do without it. That is to say, you must have sufficient self-reliance to take care of yourself, and then out of the surplus of your energy you can do for others. The man who craves friendship, and yet desires a self-centered spirit more, will never lack for friends.

If you would have friends, cultivate solitude instead of society. Drink in the ozone; bathe in the sunshine; and out in the silent night, under the stars, say to yourself again and yet again, "I am a part of all my eyes behold!" And the feeling will surely come to you that you are no mere interloper between earth and sky; but that you are a necessary particle of the Whole. No harm can come to you that does not come to all, and if you shall go down, it can only be amid a wreck of worlds.

Thus by laying hold on the forces of the Universe, you are strong with them. And when you realize this, all else is easy, for in your arteries course red corpuscles, and in your heart there is the will to do and be. Carry your chin in, and the crown of your head high. We are gods in the chrysalis.

Initiative

Love, Life, and Work, 1906.

The world bestows its big prizes, both in money and honors, for but one thing. And that is Initiative. What is Initiative? I'll tell you: It is doing the right thing without being told. But next to doing the right thing without being told is to do it when you are told once. That is to say, carry the Message to Garcia! There are those who never do a thing until they are told twice: such get no honors and small pay. Next, there are those who do the right thing only when necessity kicks them from behind, and these get indifference instead of honors, and a pittance for pay.

This kind spends most of its time polishing a bench with a hard-luck story. Then, still lower down in the scale than this, we find the fellow who will not do the right thing even when someone goes along to show him how, and stays to see that he does it; he is always out of a job, and receives the contempt he deserves, unless he has a rich Pa, in which case Destiny awaits nearby with a stuffed club. To which class do you belong?

One-Man Power

Love, Life, and Work, 1906.

Every successful concern is the result of a One-Man Power. Cooperation, technically, is an iridescent dream—things cooperate because the man makes them. He cements them by his will.

But find this Man, and get his confidence, and his weary eyes will look into yours and the cry of his heart shall echo in your ears. "O, for some one to help me bear this burden!"

Then he will tell you of his endless search for Ability, and of his continual disappointments and thwartings in trying to get some one to help himself by helping him.

Ability is the one crying need of the hour. The banks are bulging with money, and everywhere are men looking for work. The harvest is ripe. But the Ability to captain the unemployed and utilize the capital, is lacking—sadly lacking. In every city there are many five- and ten-thousand-dollar-a-year positions to be filled, but the only applicants are men who want jobs at fifteen dollars a week. Your man of Ability has a place already. Yes, Ability is a rare article.

But there is something that is much scarcer, something finer far, something rarer than this quality of Ability.

It is the ability to recognize Ability.

The sternest comment that ever can be made against employers as a class, lies in the fact that men of Ability usually succeed in showing their worth in spite of their employer, and not with his assistance and encouragement.

If you know the lives of men of Ability, you know that they discovered their power, almost without exception, thru chance or accident. Had the accident not occurred that made the opportunity, the man would have remained unknown and practically lost to the world. The experience of Tom Potter, telegraph operator at an obscure little way station, is truth painted large. That fearful night, when most of the wires were down and a passenger train went through the bridge, gave Tom Potter the opportunity of discovering himself. He took charge of the dead, cared for the wounded, settled fifty claims—drawing drafts on the company—burned the last vestige of the wreck, sunk the waste iron in the river and repaired the bridge before the arrival of the Superintendent on the spot.

"Who gave you the authority to do all this?" demanded the Superintendent.

"Nobody," replied Tom, "I assumed the authority."

The next month Tom Potter's salary was five thousand dollars a year, and in three years he was making ten times this, simply because he could get other men to do things.

Why wait for an accident to discover Tom Potter? Let us set traps for Tom Potter, and lie in wait for him. Perhaps Tom Potter is just around the corner, across the street, in the next room, or at our elbow. Myriads of embryonic Tom Potters await discovery and development if we but look for them.

I know a man who roamed the woods and fields for thirty years and never found an Indian arrow. One day he began to think "arrow," and stepping out of his doorway he picked one up. Since then he has collected a bushel of them.

Suppose we cease wailing about incompetence, sleepy indifference and slipshod "help" that watches the clock. These things exist—let us dispose of the subject by admitting it, and then emphasize the fact that freckled farmer boys come out of the West and East and often go to the front and do things in a masterly way. There is one name that stands out in history like a beacon light after all these twenty-five hundred years have passed, just because the man had the sublime genius of discovering Ability. That man is Pericles. Pericles made Athens.

And to-day the very dust of the streets of Athens is being sifted and searched for relics and remnants of the things made by people who were captained by men of Ability who were discovered by Pericles.

There is very little competition in this line of discovering Ability. We sit down and wail because Ability does not come our way. Let us think "Ability," and possibly we can jostle Pericles there on his pedestal, where he has stood for over a score of centuries—the man with a supreme genius for recognizing Ability. Hail to thee, Pericles, and hail to thee, Great Unknown, who shall be the first to successfully imitate this captain of men.

The Master Man

The Book of Business, 1913.

Industry is intelligent action, motion, movement. And now science tells us that thought also is a physical action, a movement, a vibration of the cells of the brain. Wandering, dreamy thought is merely bad habit, or, more properly, lack of a good habit, for it leads nowhere.

To carry bricks back and forth from one side of the street to the other is not industry, because it lacks intelligent purpose.

To think and make no headway is simply to carry bricks back and forth.

To play the devil's tattoo on a chair; monkey with the forks and spoons at table; adjust your necktie forty times a minute; stroke your mustache or hitch your trousers—these things are not industry. Gents do these things, but gentlemen never. And the difference between the gent and the gentleman is the difference between the Man and the Master Man. The Master Man is simply a man who is master of one person—himself.

When you have mastered yourself, you are Bthen fit to take charge of other people. The Master Man is a person who has evolved Intelligent Industry, Concentration, Self-Confidence, until these things become the habit of his life.

Industry in its highest sense means conscious, useful and intelligent effort. Carried to a certain point, Industry is healthful stimulation—it means active circulation, good digestion, sound sleep.

The sensible man will ascertain his limitations and not carry his industry to the point of exhaustion. Before he is tired out, he will turn his attention to something else. The ability to concentrate requires the ability to relax. In order to work you must know how to play. Men who carry great burdens and responsibilities are always those who are able at times to lay down the burden and be a child with the children. They can laugh. And there is no medicine equal to the merry laugh.

It is the intermittent current that makes the telephone possible; the man of power is the man who changes his work—he does one thing at a time, but he does not do the thing all the time.

To cultivate concentration, practice relaxation. Lie down on the floor for three minutes on your back, breathe deeply, lie still, and turn your mind in—thinking of nothing. To concentrate on your work you must enjoy your work. And to enjoy your work you must drop it at certain hours. He lasts longest, and soars highest, who cultivates the habit of just being a boy for an hour a day. Take a vacation every day if you want to do good work.

Are you in the treadmill? Well, the only way you can get out is by evolving mastership.

We are controlled by our habits. At first we manage them, but later they manage us. Habits young are like lion's cubs—so fluffy and funny! Have a care what kind of habits you are evolving—soon you will be in their power, and they may eat you up. It is habit that chains us to the treadmill and makes us subject to the will of others. And it is habit that gives mastership—of yourself and others.

Industry is a habit. Men who go to bed any old time and get up when they feel like it are never industrious—worse, they are never healthy. Muldoon says that the man who has to get up at six o'clock in the morning never has insomnia. If you have to get up at six, you'll go to bed at ten, and this means you'll get the habit of going to sleep.

If you acquire the habit of studying and reading good books from seven-thirty to nine-thirty six evenings a week you'll soon find it a delightful habit.

I know a great writer in England who writes every morning from eight o'clock to eleven, and he writes at no other time. He has acquired the habit. At eight o'clock his brain begins to fire up, and he finds it easy and pleasurable—necessary—to concentrate on his work.

The habit of Self-Confidence is a result of the habits of Industry and Concentration. And I hope I've made it clear that Concentration is the result of pleasurable, useful effort or Industry.

Also I hope I've made it clear that for Industry to be of the first quality, the person must at times relax and find rest in change through play—be a child—run, frolic, dig in the garden, saw wood—relax.

When you have reached a point where your work gives you a great, quiet joy, and through this joy and interest you concentrate, then comes Self-Confidence. You are now well out on the road to Mastership.

Robert Louis Stevenson said, "I know what pleasure is, for I have done good work."

The recipe for Self-Confidence is: Do good work. "Courage," says Emerson, "comes from having done the thing before."

A man who does good work does not have to talk, apologize or explain—his work speaks. And even though there be no one to appreciate it, the man feels in it a great, quiet joy. He relaxes, smiles, rests, fully intent on taking up his labors tomorrow and doing better than ever. The highest reward that God gives us for doing good work is the ability to do better work. Rest means rust.

So we get the formula: Acquire and evolve physical and mental industry by doing certain things at certain hours, ceasing the effort before it becomes wearisome. In mental work keep in touch with people who are a little beyond you.

The joy and satisfaction of successful effort—overcoming obstacles, getting lessons, mastering details which we once thought difficult—evolves into a habit, and gives Concentration. Industry and Concentration and Self-Confidence spell Mastership.

So from the man we get the Master Man, What lies beyond I do not know. Perhaps when I become a Master I shall know—one stage at a time is enough. If there isn't time in this life, perhaps there will be hereafter.

The Boy from Missouri Valley

The Philistine, July 1902.

Well, it wasn't so very long ago—only about twenty-three years.

I was foreman of a factory, and he lived a thousand miles away, at Missouri Valley, Iowa. I was twenty-four, and he was fourteen. His brother was traveling for the Firm, and one day this brother showed me a letter from the lad in Missouri Valley. The missive was so painstaking, so exact, and revealed the soul of the child so vividly, that I laughed aloud—a laugh that died away to a sigh.

The boy was beating his wings against the bars—the bars of Missouri Valley—he wanted opportunity. And all he got was unending toil, dead monotony, stupid misunderstanding, and corn-bread and molasses.

There wasn't love enough in Missouri Valley to go 'round—that was plain. The boy's mother had been of the Nancy Hanks type—worn, yellow and sad—and had given up the fight and been left to sleep her long sleep in a prairie grave on one of the many migrations. The father's ambition had got stuck in the mud, and under the tongue-lash of a strident, strenuous, gee-haw consort, he had run up the white flag.

The boy wanted to come East.

It was a dubious investment—a sort of financial plunge, a blind pool—to send for this buckwheat midget. The fare was thirty-three dollars and fifty cents.

The Proprietor, a cautious man, said that the boy wasn't worth the money. There were plenty of boys—the alleys swarmed with them.

So there the matter rested.

But the lad in Missouri Valley didn't let it rest long. He had been informed that we did not consider him worth thirty-three dollars and fifty cents, so he offered to split the difference. He would come for half—he could ride on half-fare—the Railroad Agent at Missouri Valley said that if he bought a half-fare ticket, got on a train, and explained to the conductor and everybody that he was 'leven, goin' on twelve, and stuck to it, it would be all right; and he would not expect any wages until he had paid us back. He had no money of his own, all he earned was taken from him by the kind folks with whom he lived, and would be until noon of the day he was twenty-one years old. Did we want to invest sixteen dollars and seventy-five cents in him?

We waxed reckless and sent the money—more than that, we sent a twenty-dollar bill. We plunged!

In just a week the investment arrived. He did not advise when he would come, or how. He came, we saw, he conquered. Why should he advise of his coming? He just reported, and his first words were the

Duke's motto: "I am here."

He was unnecessarily freckled and curiously small. His legs had the Greek curve, from much horseback riding, herding cattle on the prairies; his hair was the color of a Tamworth pig; his hands were red; his wrists bony and briar-scarred. He carried his shoes in his hands, so as not to wear out the sidewalk, or because they aggravated sundry stone-bruises—I don't know which.

"I am here!" said the lad, and he planked down on the desk three dollars and twenty-five cents. It was the change from the twenty-dollar bill. "Didn't you have to spend any money on the way here?" I asked.

"No, I had all I wanted to eat," he replied, and pointed to a basket that sat on the floor.

I called in the Proprietor, and we looked the lad over. We walked around him twice, gazed at each other, and adjourned to the hallway for consultation.

The boy was not big enough to do a man's work, and if we set him to work in the factory with the city boys, they would surely pick on him and make life for him very uncomfortable. He had a half-sad and winsome look that had won from our hard hearts something akin to pity. He was so innocent, so full of faith, and we saw at a glance that he had been overworked, underfed—at least misfed—and underloved. He was different from other boys—and in spite of the grime of travel, and the freckles, he was pretty as a ground-squirrel.

His faith made him whole: he won us. But why had we brought him to the miserable and dirty city—this grim place of disillusionment! "He might index the letter-book?" I ventured. "That's it, yes, let him index the letter-book." So I went back and got the letter-book. But the boy's head only came to the top of the stand-up desk, and when he reached for the letter-book on the desk he had to grope for it. I gave him my high-stool, but this was too low.

"I know what to do," he said. Through the window that looked from the office to the shipping-room, he had espied a pile of boxes. "I know what to do!"

In a minute he had placed two boxes end to end, nailed them together, clinched the nails, and carried his improvised high-stool into the office.

I know what to do!

"And he usually did; and does yet.

We found him a boarding-place with a worthy widow whose children had all grown big and flown. Her house was empty, and so was her mother-heart: she was like that old woman in *Rab*, who was placed on the surgeon's table and given chloroform, and who held to her breast an imaginary child, and crooned a lullaby to a babe, dead thirty years before.

So the boy boarded with the widow and worked in the office.

He indexed the letter-book—he indexed everything. And then he filed everything—letters, bills, circulars. He stamped the letters going out, swept the office, and dusted things that had never been dusted before. He was orderly, alert, active, cheerful, and the Proprietor said to me one day, "I wonder how we ever got along without that boy from Missouri Valley!"

Six months had passed, and there came a day when one of the workmen intimated to the Proprietor that he better look out for that red-headed office-boy.

Of course, the Proprietor insisted on hearing the rest, and the man then explained that almost every night the boy came back to the office. He had seen him. The boy had a tin box and letter-books in it, and papers, and the Lord knows what not!

Watch him!

The Proprietor advised with me because I was astute—at least he thought I was, and I agreed with him.

He thought Jabesh was at the bottom of it.

Jabesh was our chief competitor. Jabesh had hired away two of our men, and we had gotten three of his. "Jabe," we called him in derision—Jabe had gotten into the factory twice on pretense of seeing a man who wanted to join the Epworth League or Something. We had ordered him out, because we knew he was trying to steal our "process." Jabe was a rogue —that was sure.

Worse than that, Jabe was a Methodist. The Proprietor was a Baptist, and regarded all Methodists with a prenatal aversion that swung between fear and contempt. The mere thought of Jabe gave us gooseflesh. Jabesh was the bugaboo that haunted our dreams. Our chief worry was that we would never be able to save our Bank-Balance alive, for fear o' Jabe.

"That tarnashun Jabe has hired our office-boy to give him a list of our customers—he is stealing our formulas, I know," said the Proprietor. "The cub's pretense of wanting a key to the factory so he could sweep out early was really that he might get in late."

Next day we watched the office-boy. He surely looked guilty—his freckles stood out like sunspots, and he was more bow-legged than ever.

The workman who had given the clue, on being further interrogated, was sure he had seen Jabe go by the factory twice in one evening.

That settled it.

At eight o'clock that night we went down to the factory. It was a full mile, and in an "objectionable" part of the town. There was a dim light in the office. We peered through the windows, and sure enough, there was the boy hard at work writing. There were several books before him, a tin box and some papers. We waited and watched him copy something into a letter-book.

We withdrew and consulted. To confront the culprit then and there seemed the proper thing. We unlocked the door and walked softly in.

The boy was startled by our approach, and still more by our manner. When the Proprietor demanded the letter that he had just written, he began to cry, and then we knew we had him.

The Proprietor took the letter and read it. It was to Jimmy Smith in Missouri Valley. It told all about how the writer was getting on, about the good woman he boarded with, and it told all about me and about the Proprietor. It pictured us as models of virtue, excellence and truth.

But we were not to be put off thus. We examined the letter-book, and alas! it was filled only with news-letters to sundry cousins and aunts. Then we dived to the bottom of the tin box, still in search of things contraband. All we found was a little old Bible, a diary, and some trinkets in the way of lace and a ribbon that had once been the property of the dead Nancy Hanks.

Then we found a Savings-Bank Book, and by the entries saw that the boy had deposited one dollar every Monday morning for eleven weeks. He had been with us for six months, and his pay was two dollars a week and board—we wondered what he had done with the rest!

We questioned the offender at length. The boy averred that he came to the office evenings only because he wanted to write letters and get his 'rithmetic lesson. He would not think of writing his personal letters on our time, and the only reason he wanted to write at the office instead of at home was so he could use the letter-press. He wanted to copy all of his letters—one should be businesslike in all things.

The Proprietor coughed and warned the boy never to let it happen again. We started for home, walking silently but very fast.

The stillness was broken only once, when the Proprietor said: "That consarned Jabe! If ever I find him around our factory, I'll tweak his nincompoop nose, that's what I will do."

Twenty-three years! That factory has grown to be the biggest of its kind in America. The red-haired boy from Missouri Valley is its manager. Emerson says, "Every great institution is the lengthened shadow of a single man." The Savings-Bank Habit came naturally to that boy from Missouri Valley. In a year he was getting six dollars and board, and he deposited four dollars every Monday. In three years this had increased to ten, and some years after, when he became a partner, he had his limit in the Bank. The Savings-Bank Habit is not so bad as the Cab Habit—nor so costly to your thinkery and wallet as the Cigarette Habit.

I have been wage-earner, foreman and employer. I have had a thousand men on my payroll at a time, and I'll tell you this: The man with the Savings-Bank Habit is the one who never gets laid off: he's the one who can get along without you, but you can not get along without him. The Savings-Bank Habit means sound sleep, good digestion, cool judgment and manly independence. The most healthful thing I know of is a Savings-Bank Book—there are no microbes in it to steal away your peace of mind. It is a guarantee of good behavior.

The Missouri Valley boy gets twenty-five thousand a year, they say. It is none too much. Such masterly men are rare; Rockefeller says he has vacancies for eight now, with salaries no object, if they can do the work.

That business grew because the boy from Missouri Valley grew with it, and he grew because the business grew. Which is a free paraphrase from Macaulay, who said that Horace Walpole influenced his age because he was influenced by his age. Jabesh has gone on his Long Occasion, discouraged and whipped by an unappreciative world. Jabe never acquired the Savings-Bank Habit. If he had had the gumption to discover a red-haired boy from Missouri Valley, he might now be sporting an automobile on Delaware Avenue instead of being in Abraham's Bosom.

We shall all be in Abraham's Bosom day after tomorrow; and then I'll explain to Jabesh that no man ever succeeded in a masterly way, excepting as he got levelheaded men with the Savings-Bank Habit to do his work. Blessed is that man who has found somebody to do his work.

There is plenty of iron pyrites, but the Proprietor and I know Pay-Gravel when we see it.

I guess so!

A Prayer

Love, Life, and Work, 1906.

The supreme prayer of my heart is not to be learned, rich, famous, powerful, or "good," but simply to be radiant. I desire to radiate health, cheerfulness, calm courage and good will. I wish to live without hate, whim, jealousy, envy, fear. I wish to be simple, honest, frank, natural, clean in mind and clean in body, unaffected—ready to say "I do not know," if it be so, and to meet all men on an absolute equality—to face any obstacle and meet every difficulty unabashed and unafraid.

I wish others to live their lives, too—up to their highest, fullest and best. To that end I pray that I may never meddle, interfere, dictate, give advice that is not wanted, or assist when my services are not needed. If I can help people, I'll do it by giving them a chance to help themselves; and if I can uplift or inspire, let it be by example, inference, and suggestion, rather than by injunction and dictation. That is to say, I desire to be radiant—to radiate life.

THE END

www.ingramcontent.com/pod-product-compliance
Lightning Source LLC
Chambersburg PA
CBHW050912120626
46552CB00004B/1537